B·E·A·U·T·I·F·U·L
O·L·D
A·L·P·H·A·B·E·T·S

Designs & Stitches

J U T T A · L A M M È R

Sterling Publishing Co. Inc. New York
Distributed in the U.K. by Blandford Press

By the same author:

Making Samplers: New & Traditional Designs

Translated by Hannah Meyer
Edited and adapted by Vilma Liacouras Chantiles

Library of Congress Cataloging in Publication Data

Lammèr, Jutta.
  Beautiful old alphabets.

  Translation of: Schöne alte Alphabete zum Nachsticken.
  Includes index.
  1. Embroidery—Patterns. 2. Alphabets. I. Title.
TT773.L3513   1984   746.3'041   84-2764
ISBN 0-8069-5534-1
ISBN 0-8069-7892-9 (pbk.)

Contents

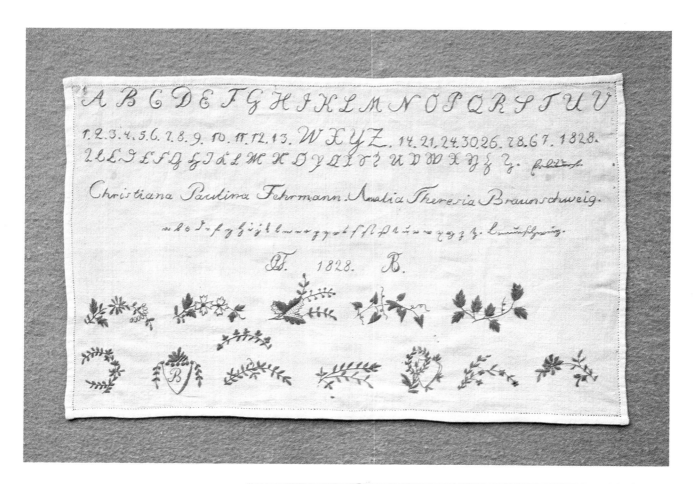

(Above) **1** Sampler from 1828. Letters are embroidered in stem stitch and the ornamental sprays are worked in satin stitch.

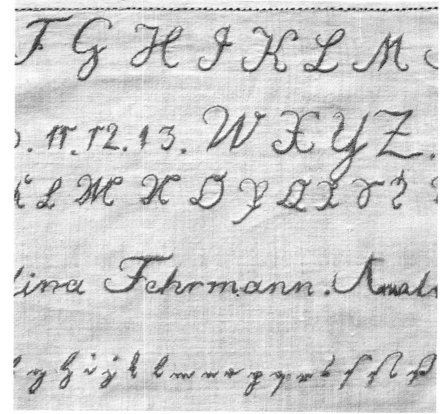

(Right) **2** This detail illustrates the original lines of the letters. The letters may have been embroidered freehand without a pattern.

Alphabets and Stitchery

Embroidering white linen with colored threads is an art that has been known since the fourteenth century. The marking of laundry with embroidered letters or monograms at first had only a practical purpose: It helped identify the pieces laid out for bleaching. Gradually, the embroidering of alphabets developed into an art, in which women—the poor as well as affluent—competed with

Folk Art Revived

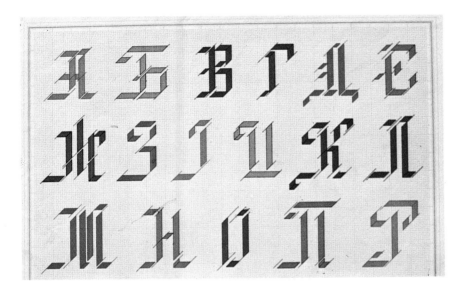

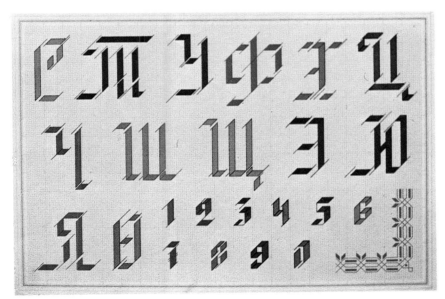

3 Embroidering letters, monograms and entire alphabets is an international handicraft. Left, a two-part embroidery pattern from Greece is illustrated.

each other. The basic shapes of the letters were developed and often altered in form and adorned with scrolls. Cross stitch was worked according to the weave of the linen. Satin stitch gained in popularity and was used with the stem stitch for the finely curved beginning and ending of many letters. Frequently, satin stitch was embroidered using a single thread on the finest weave and then edged in stem stitch.

In the eighteenth century, the cross stitch was worked almost entirely in white embroidery—satin and stem stitches embroidered with white threads on white fabric—in the style of peasant needlework.

At the beginning of the nineteenth century, the embroidering of alphabets and letters experienced a renaissance. Magazines, such as *Bazar* and *Modenwelt* (*Style World*), published patterns for embroidery in nearly all issues; many of these patterns are shown in this book. Eager needlework teachers developed new forms of letters and personally published small pamphlets. For example, several alphabets from these publications are illustrated in this book. Unfortunately, the original patterns are not all in perfect condition; consequently, reproductions from them are also imperfect.

In early times, embroidery was more popular with small, single motifs: letters, monograms and letter combinations. Not limited only to bed and table linens, these letters were used on all textiles, on place cards, jewelry, greeting cards, or even on umbrellas! At the same time, of course, embroidering entire alphabets flourished. These alphabet samplers were beautifully framed and hung on the wall.

This book offers many beautiful letters from the eighteenth and nineteenth centuries. Their shapes originated during an even earlier time, however. Everyone can find the right pattern—from the heavy *A* to the dainty *Z*—for counted or free style embroideries.

All crosses, four-sided stitches or other symbols can be transferred by counting the threads of the evenweave. Every symbol stands for a cross stitch, a four-sided stitch, or other stitch. These embroideries may be worked either on evenweave embroidery fabrics (warp and filling threads are woven symmetrically), or on finely woven fabrics with a soft, waste canvas (evenweave canvas). Baste the waste canvas to the fabric that will be embroidered. After basting the canvas to the fabric, you embroider through both the canvas and fabric following the desired pattern or chart. When you have completed the embroidery, carefully pull out the canvas threads with tweezers (Illustrations 4 and 5).

Counting Patterns

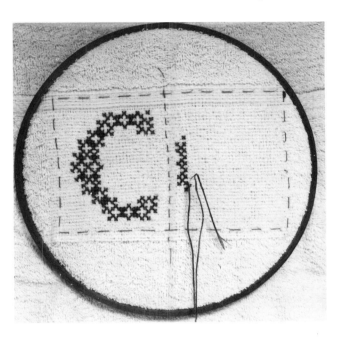

4 Counted embroideries, such as cross stitch, can be worked on finely woven (not evenweave) fabric. Baste waste canvas on the fabric and embroider carefully with the needle precisely at right angles to the work.

5 The waste canvas threads are removed, one at a time, after the embroidery is completed.

Letters that cannot be embroidered on evenweave fabrics must be transferred from the pattern to the fabric. This can be done by drawing the motif on tracing paper and transferring, using transfer paper (not carbon paper) available at hobby or needlework shops. The edges of the letters are sharper if you use a transfer pencil on the back of the drawing and iron the lines with a hot or warm iron (Illustrations 6, 7 and 8). After embroidering, any visible lines can be washed out.

Drawing Patterns

6   To transfer a letter onto the fabric: Cover the pattern with tracing paper; secure the edges, and trace the letter with a ball-point pen.

7   Remove the transparent drawing from the pattern, turn and trace again on the back with a transfer pencil (available in hobby and needlework shops).

8   Pin the tracing paper (with the drawing on the back) to the embroidery fabric. With a hot or warm iron transfer the pattern to the fabric, using the appropriate temperature.

In counted embroideries or those that are worked over a counting aid, such as waste canvas, the size of the letter can be determined by the count of the weave as well as by how many threads used for each stitch or half stitch. Examples are illustrated below.

Planning Embroidered Letters

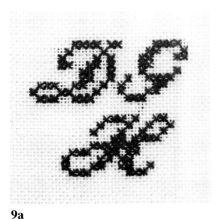

9a

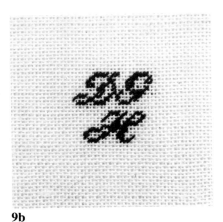

9b

9a Cross stitch over 2 warp (lengthwise) threads and 2 filling (horizontal) threads, embroidered on linen number 10.5 gives a letter height of about ⅝ inch (18 mm).

9b Half cross stitch over 1 thread in height (warp) and width (filling), also embroidered on linen number 10.5, produces a letter height of about ⅜ inch (1 cm).

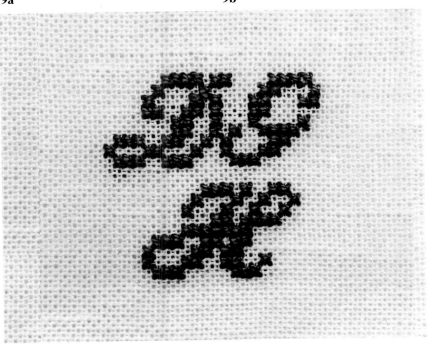

9c

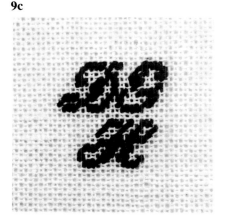

9d

9c Cross stitch embroidered as 9a on linen number 7 produces a letter height of about 1 inch (26 mm).

9d Half cross stitch embroidered on linen number 7 produces a letter height of ½ inch (13 mm).

The most practical linen even-weaves are numbers 12 (12 threads per ⅜ inch or 1 cm) and 7 (7 threads per ⅜ inch or 1 cm).

9

Cross stitch is not appropriate for monograms embroidered with overlapping letters. If the cross stitch must be used for a monogram, however, embroider the initial of the first name in a lighter thread color and slightly longer size than the second initial. The initial of the last name should be worked in a darker color slightly wider than the first. Choose an alphabet with letters that lend themselves easily to widening or lengthening. Where the embroidery overlaps, omit the cross stitches of the first letter in favor of the second.

Letters that are not counted on evenweave using a counting pattern but have to be transferred may easily be enlarged using a photocopier. If the letters are produced in the negative and remain unembroidered, mark the letter outline and embroider around it (Illustration 10).

10 In this design, only the background is worked and the letter is not embroidered, to produce a negative letter.

Embroidery Technique

Embroideries on finely woven fabrics that cannot be counted can be worked more easily in an embroidery frame. When securing the fabric, be careful that the weave is exactly at right angles. Counted embroideries on linen evenweave can be done without a frame. Pull the embroidery thread evenly and not too tightly.

Embroider with a dull-pointed needle, corresponding to the thickness of the embroidery thread. The needle should never be thinner than the thread. To prevent the working thread from roughening, use a shorter thread than usual and change to a new thread frequently. While embroidering, avoid twisting the embroidery thread. Continually control the thread and adjust it as you embroider. For example, when working with pearl cotton thread, the twist may loosen; twist it again before continuing. When working with multi-strand threads, the opposite is true; the parallel threads get twisted and must be straightened by laying them flat.

Select any embroidery fabric and embroidery thread that you prefer. It is important that the fabric weave and the embroidery thread are of a similar texture, especially when embroidering on knitted fabrics. Before embroidering, test the background fabric and the embroidery thread to be sure they are colorfast.

Letters in this book are embroidered using the following stitches: cross stitch, four-sided stitch, double running or Holbein stitch, cross stitch (simple, two-sided and with four-sided stitch in back), star eyelet stitch (counting stitches suitable to use with counting patterns), as well as satin stitch, stem stitch, feather stitch, chain stitch and wave stitch. Instead of satin stitches, you can also work chain stitches vertically in close rows. For embroideries on knitted fabrics, the wave stitch is most suitable; it can also be worked following a counting pattern (one symbol equals one wave stitch).

There are several ways to embroider cross stitches. The different cross stitches can be identified by looking at the back of the embroidery. Simple cross stitch has vertical or horizontal running stitches on the back; the two-sided cross stitch shows the same stitches on the front and back sides, and the four-sided stitch, worked in reverse, shows the crosses on the front and a four-sided stitch (square) on the back. The four-sided stitch can be worked from the front when squares are preferred. Several alphabets of this book illustrate a combination of these stitches.

Embroidery Stitches

Cross stitch—simple: The simple cross stitch consists of 2 crossing half stitches, usually covering 2 warp and filling threads of the evenweave fabric. The bottom stitches run from lower left to upper right, and the covering stitch from lower right to upper left (Illustrations 11a and 11b).

Cross Stitch— Simple

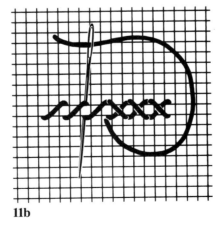

11a   11b

Cross stitch—two-sided: Two-sided cross stitch is reversible. It includes a bottom stitch, half stitch and cover stitch. The bottom stitch goes from lower left to upper right (12a); a half stitch from center to lower right (12b); and a cover stitch from lower right to upper left (12c). If you continue the row to the right, repeat the

Cross Stitch— Two-sided

movements (12d). To continue in a downward direction, the lower stitch moves from upper right to lower left (12e); a half stitch from center to lower right (12f); and the cover stitch from lower right to upper left, bringing needle out at lower right. To continue left, work the lower stitch from upper right to lower left (12e); work the half stitch from center to upper left (12g); and cover stitch from lower right to upper left (12h). To move diagonally to the right, make a half stitch from center to lower left (12i); cover with full stitch from lower left to upper right; a half stitch from center to lower right and cover stitch from lower right to upper left. Work half stitches to position your needle for direction of the next stitch. (12j).

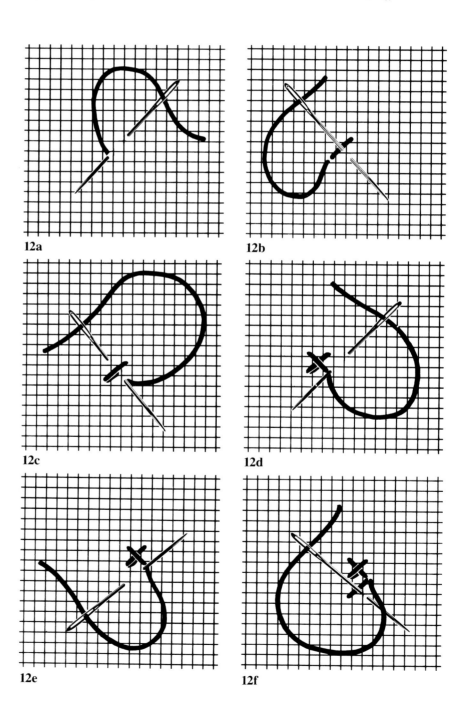

12a

12b

12c

12d

12e

12f

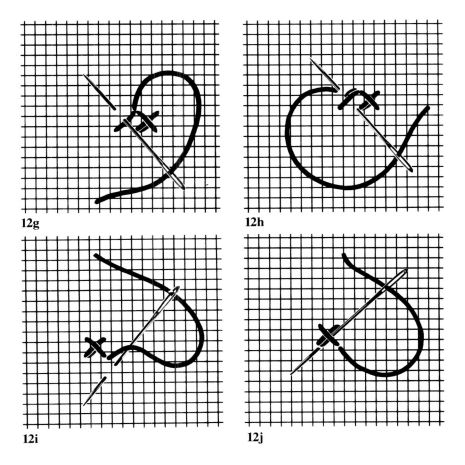

12g 12h 12i 12j

Cross and four-sided stitch: The four-sided stitch produces a cross on the back and a square on the front. Use this stitch for decorative effects. To make a cross on the front, working left to right, insert the needle diagonally lower right and bring needle out opposite left (13a); turn needle point downwards and insert diagonally upper right and bring out directly below (13b); insert needle diagonally left (covering the earlier diagonal stitch) and bring out below (13c). Begin a new stitch below the one just completed (13a) to complete the square in back. (You may prefer to use Illustrations 15a–15d, working on the *wrong* side of the fabric to make crosses in front.)

Cross and Four-sided Stitch

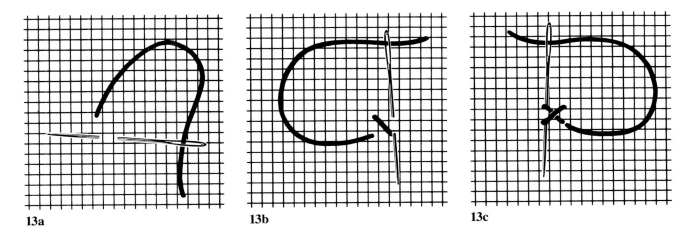

13a 13b 13c

14 Illustration of the cross and four-sided stitch: (left) worked with the four-sided stitch showing on the front side, forming crosses on the back; (right) crosses worked on the front side, forming four-sided stitches on the back. If the embroidery pattern calls for crosses not embroidered in even rows, the changes can be made by taking additional stitches in horizontal, vertical or diagonal direction to bring the needle out at the correct starting point.

Four-sided Stitch

Four-sided stitch (cross on the back): When using fine even-weave, work over 2 warp (vertical) and 2 filling (horizontal) threads. Working from right to left, insert needle 2 threads above the starting point and bring needle out diagonally opposite to the left (15a); then insert the needle to the right where the needle had emerged at the starting point, angle needle diagonally under the fabric and bring needle out at upper left (15b); insert needle opposite at upper right and bring needle out diagonally left (15c); begin a new stitch (15d) which completes the square on the back and begins a new cross on the front. Illustration 14 shows the letter *D* embroidered in four-sided stitch (left) and in cross stitch (right).

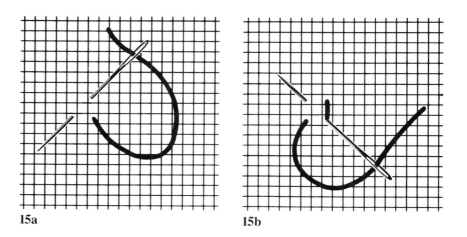

15a   15b

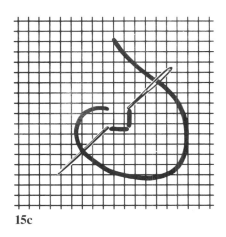

15c

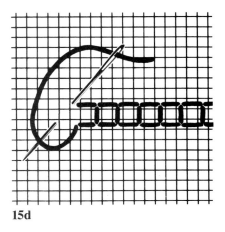

15d

Double running or Holbein stitch: Double running or Holbein stitch is useful as an outline stitch and for decorative touches. It is done in 2 journeys over the same number of threads. As shown in Illustration 16, first work the first journey in vertical stitches; on the return journey, work all the horizontal stitches.

Double Running or Holbein Stitch

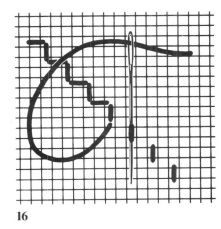

16

Double cross stitch: The double cross stitch consists of 2 cross stitches embroidered over each other. The bottom cross stitch runs diagonally, and the upper runs both vertically and horizontally (Illustrations 17a and 17b).

Double Cross Stitch

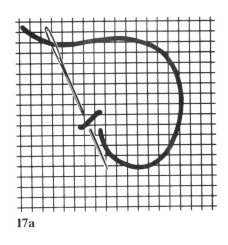

17a

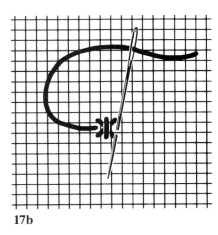

17b

18 The size of embroidered letters can be determined by the coarseness or fineness of the evenweave you use and also by the number of embroidery threads worked over with each stitch.

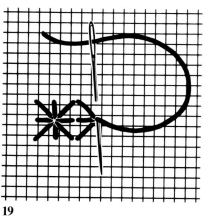

19

Star eyelet stitch: The star eyelet stitch consists of 8 consecutive stitches worked from a center hole (Illustration 19). The embroidered detail (Illustration 18) shows the variation in size by working over 1 thread or 2 threads from the center hole.

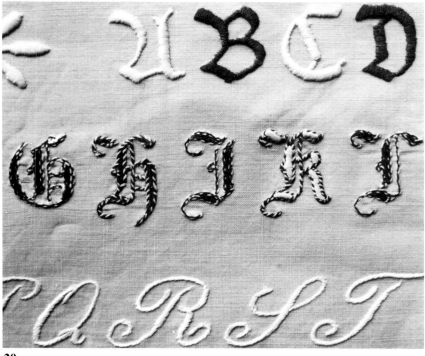

20

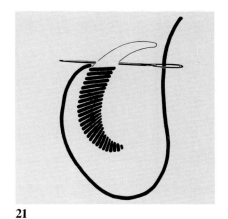

21

Satin stitch: Satin stitch can be worked on an embroidery frame. The working stitch emerges on the opposite side of the outline after bringing the needle up. Then stitch back and forth as closely as possible (Illustration 21). The stitches must completely cover the fabric without crowding. For a horizontal effect, work the stitches so that the front stitches are as horizontal as possible (Illustration 20, upper row); or for a slightly diagonal effect, work the stitches diagonally, especially for letters sloping to the right, such as italics (Illustration 20, lower row). Letters using satin stitch usually begin and end with stem stitch scrolls. Stem stitch also is used to outline satin stitch letters. Two-color outlines can be embroidered by first embroidering the outline with running stitches and then whipping or running through the stitches with a contrasting color (Illustration 22a and 22b).

22a

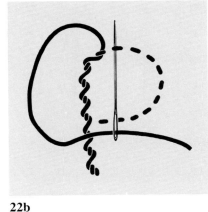

22b

20 This embroidery detail shows satin stitch embroideries with and without cord edging. The cord edging consists of running stitches which have a contrasting thread running through them, the whipped running stitch.

Stem Stitch

Stem stitch: The stem stitch can be embroidered horizontally or vertically winding to the right or to the left. To work horizontal stem stitches winding to the right, after taking the first stitch, skip several weaving threads and bring the needle up left, along the stitching line, keeping the thread down (23a). For stem stitches winding to the left, work the same but keep the working thread up (23b). To work vertical stitches, work the same as the horizontal stem stitch, laying the thread either to the left or to the right along the stitching line.

23a Stem Stitch, Winding Right

23b Stem Stitch, Winding Left

Feather Stitch

Feather stitch: Feather stitch may be worked in an embroidery frame. Working downwards, bring needle out at top center; hold the thread down with the left thumb and insert the needle a little to the right, opposite the stitch, and take a small stitch down to the center, keeping the thread under the needle. Then insert the needle slightly to the left opposite the stitch you just made and take a stitch towards the center, keeping the thread under the needle (25). Continue stitching, alternating these movements right and left; stitches may also be worked in a curved line. The working sample shows a *B*, embroidered with stem stitch and feather stitch.

24 Embroidered sample showing the letter *B* on page 90, using feather stitch and stem stitch.

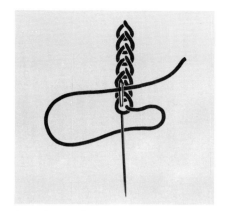

25 Feather Stitch **26 Chain Stitch**

Chain stitch: Chain stitch has many variations and can be worked in many directions. Bring needle out at the top of the line you are embroidering and hold the thread down with the thumb; insert the needle where it had last emerged and bring the needle out a short distance below or to the side, depending on your direction. Pull the thread through, keeping the thread under the needle.

Chain Stitch

Wave stitch: This is a useful stitch when working on woven or knitted fabrics. Working right to left, bring needle up at bottom center. Keeping needle pointed left in a horizontal position, insert needle above right (2 or 4 threads depending on the size of the stitch, or in the next vertical knitted row) and bring out opposite to the left (27a). To complete the stitch, insert needle where it had first emerged, keeping needle pointed left, and bring needle out in bottom center of the next position (not illustrated); continue to end of the row. To move upwards, insert needle in the above row to the left (27b).

Wave Stitch

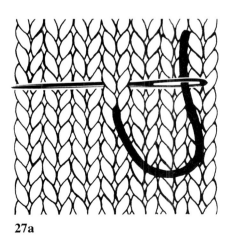

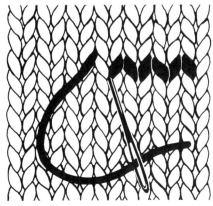

27a **27b**

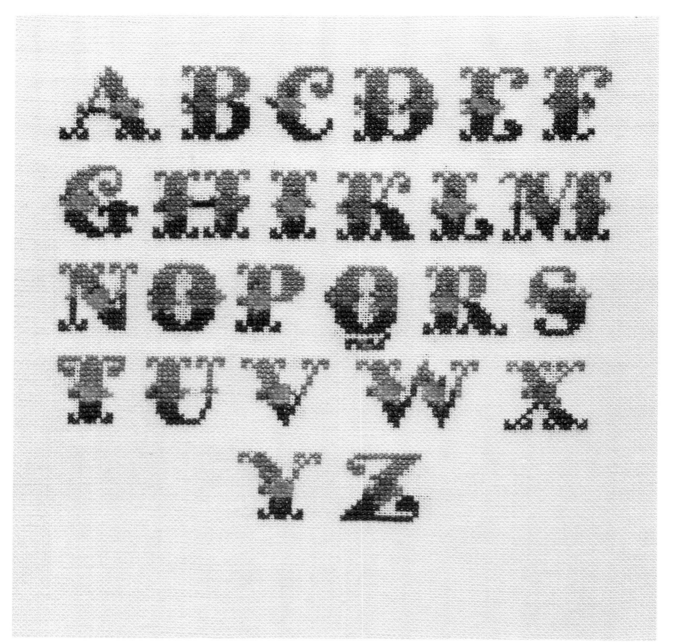

28 Cross stitch alphabet embroidered from a counting pattern from the magazine *Bazar* (page 47). The letters of the top row are a cross stitch taller than those of the four rows below.

If you wish to combine the letters of the first row with others, omit a horizontal cross stitch row on the taller letters, preferably in the upper half of the letters. The missing *J* in this alphabet can be reproduced from the left half of the letter *U* (see the enlarged counting pattern for the *U* on the cover). An embroidered sample in another color combination is found at the bottom of page 48.

Alphabet Samplers with Patterns

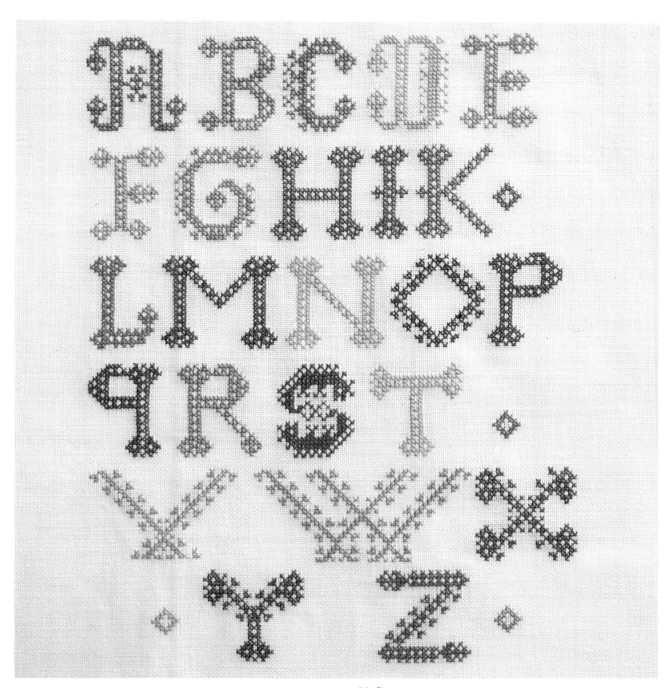

29   Embroidered on linen, this alphabet is inspired by an old German
sampler. Counting pattern is on page 22.

30 Counting pattern for the sampler on page 21, from the magazine *Modenwelt*, Berlin (1881).

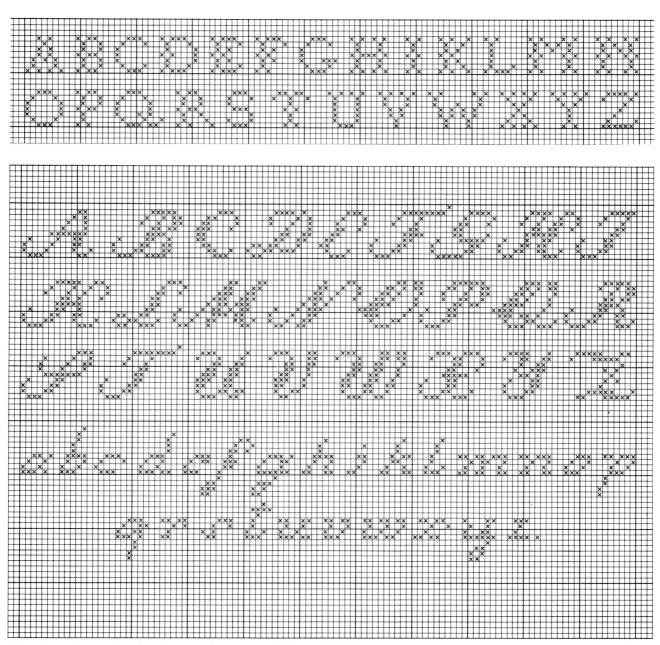

31 Counting pattern for the sampler on page 24, dated 1899.

32   An ABC sampler, typical of samplers embroidered in schools at the
turn of the century, worked in Turkey red on natural-colored linen.
Counting pattern is on page 23.

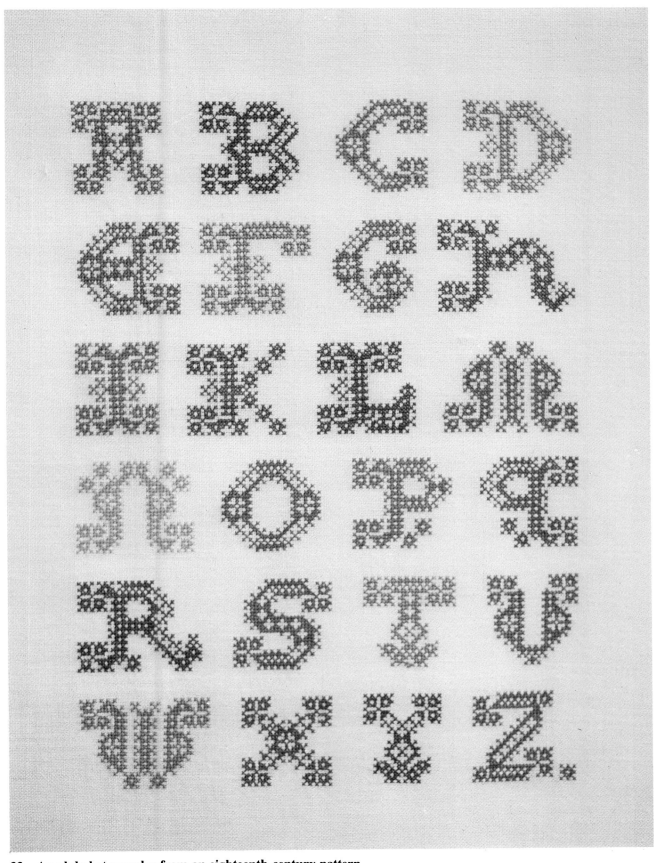

33   An alphabet sampler from an eighteenth-century pattern.

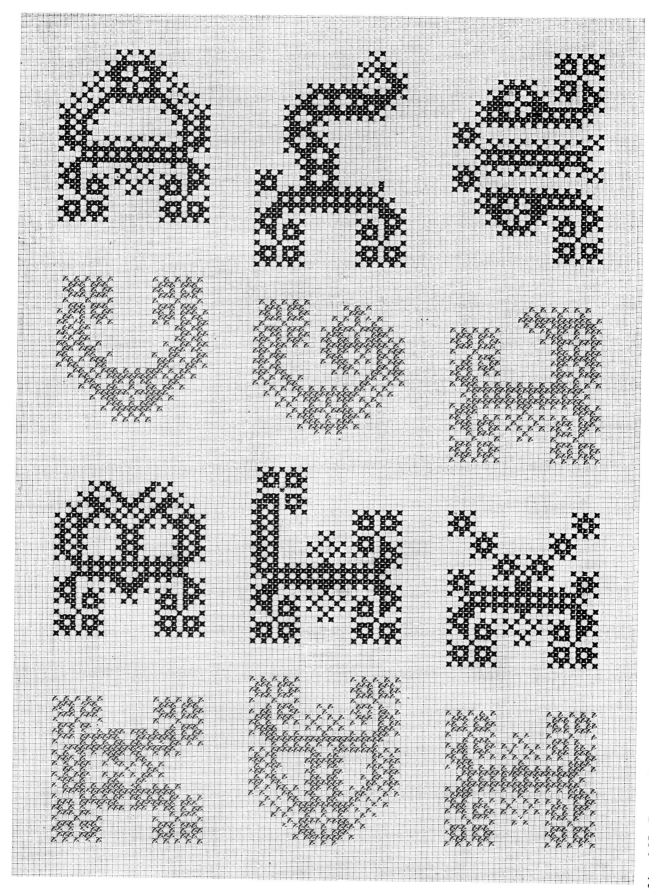

34 and 35　Pattern for the alphabet sampler on page 25, from a German linen embroidery, 1881.

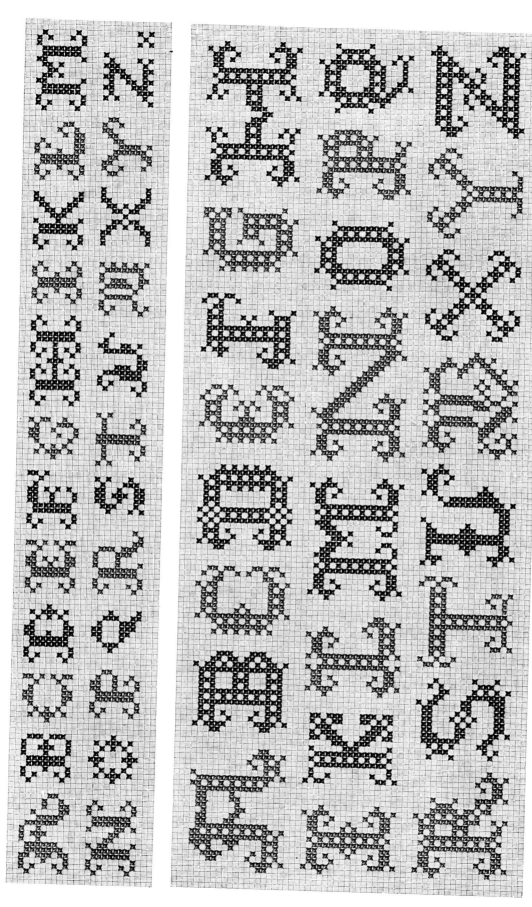

36 Two alphabets in capital letters. Working sampler is on the next page.

37 Alphabet, circa 1860, from the sampler of an old German embroidery illustrated in the magazine *Modenwelt* (1881). Early alphabets in lowercase letters are seldom found. Instead of the lowercase letters, samplers were worked in capital letters in varying sizes, as illustrated in this example. This style is found on inscriptions on monuments as well. The letter patterns provided for embroidery were often designed by the same script artists who designed inscriptions.

38 and 39   Counting pattern for the sampler on page 33.

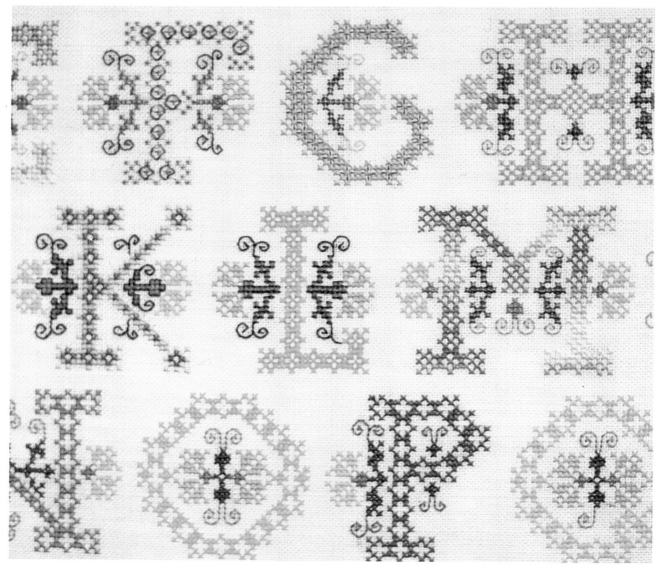

40 The beauty of the alphabet sampler on page 33 (detail above)
becomes clear only with closer observation. In certain letters, such as
the *F* and *G*, cross stitches are enhanced by straight stitches, adding
their contrasting color and a decorative touch to the embroidery.
Counting patterns are found on pages 30 and 31.

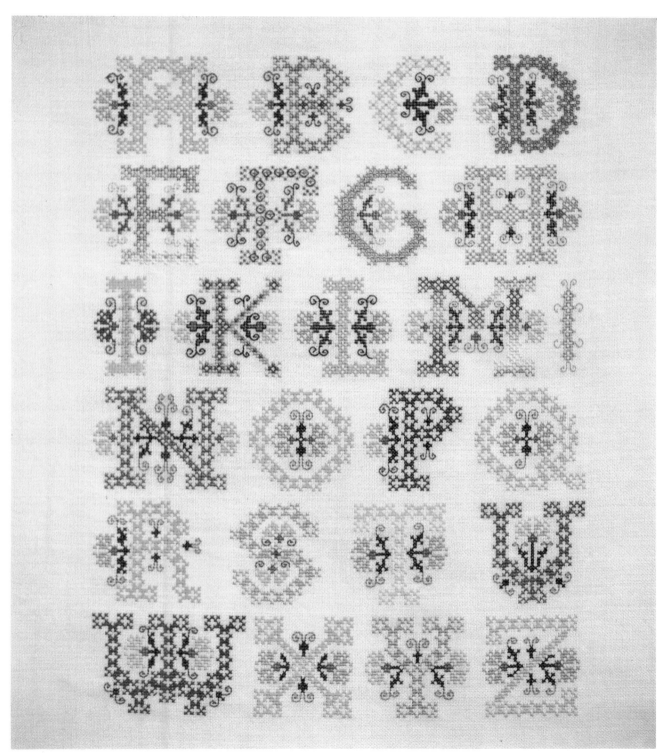

41

(Above) 42 and (Below) 43   Embroidered details of these patterns are on page 36.

44

45

46

45 to 47   Embroidered details
from the counting patterns on
page 34: XENIA (45) from alphabet b; DORIS (46) from alphabet c; *W* (47) from the
alphabet on page 35.

47

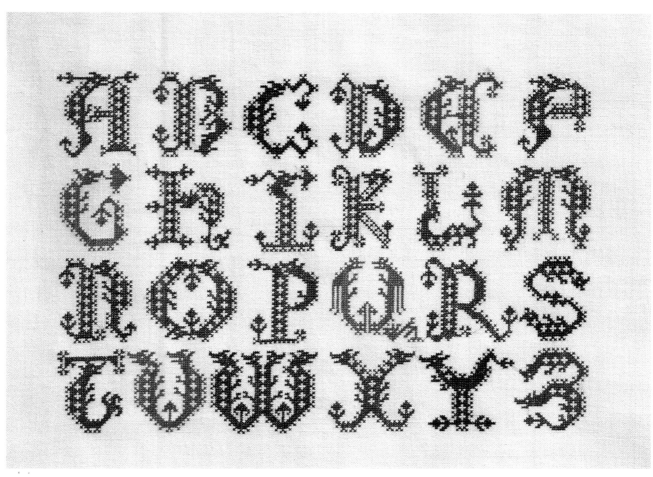

48 This mid-eighteenth-century alphabet incorporates mythical animals and stylized blossoms that are noticeable only after close observation. Each embroidered letter is like a jewelled ornament. The counting pattern is on pages 38 and 39.

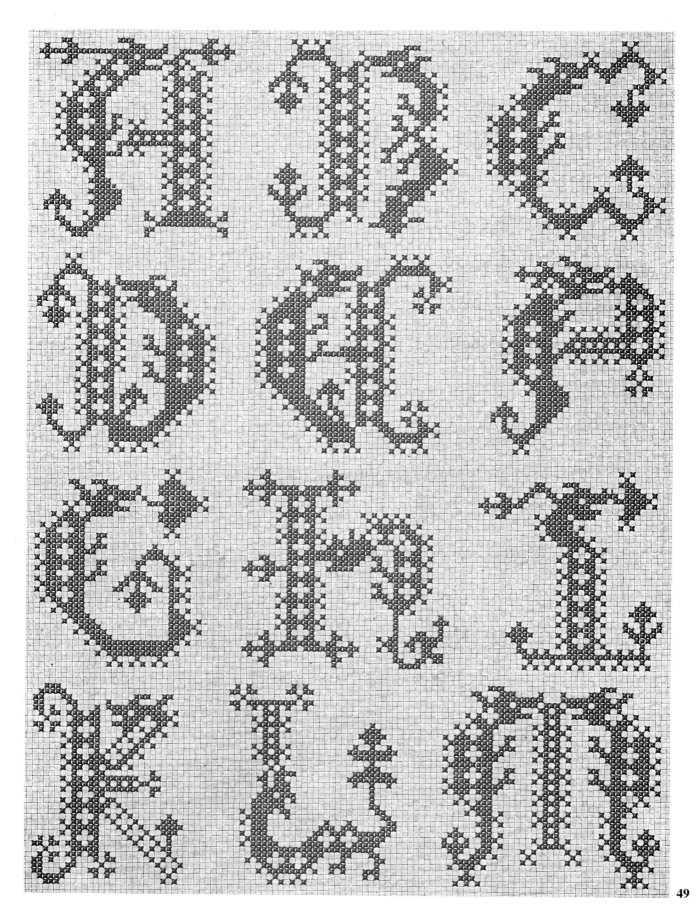

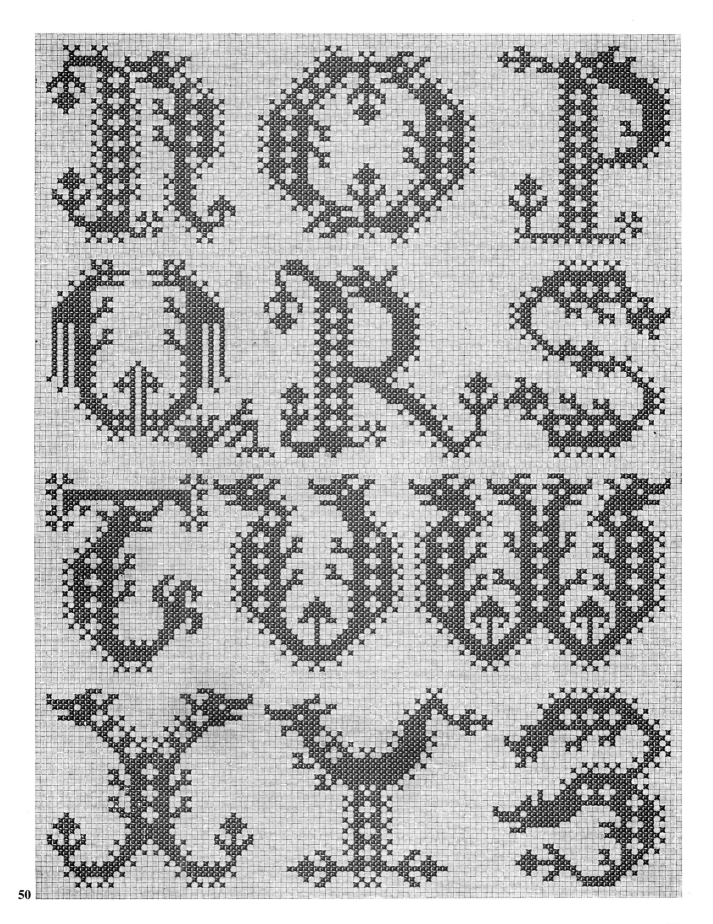

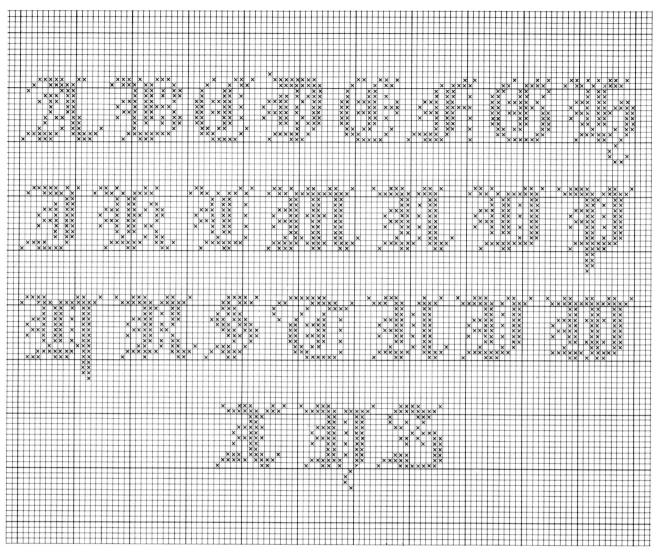

51 Counting pattern for the alphabet sampler on page 41. As in many
old samplers, the letter *I* is missing here and is replaced by the *J*. If you
need the letter *I*, reproduce it from the letter *H*, and omit the curve to
the right.

52 Alphabet sampler from south Germany embroidered on linsey-woolsey over 2 warp and filling threads with 2 strands of cotton thread. The embroidered numerals under the monograms have never been explained.

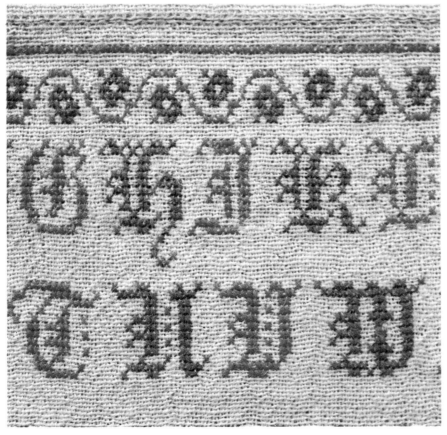

53 Detail from the alphabet sampler illustrated above. The missing *I* can be reproduced from the letter *H* by omitting the curve.

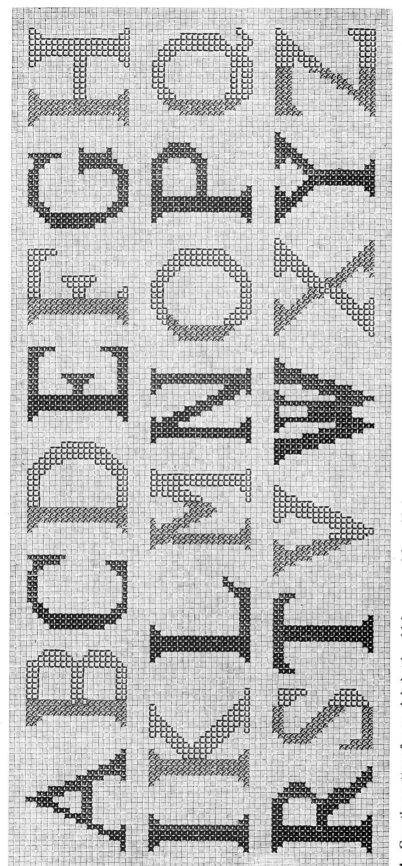

54 Counting pattern for an alphabet in which cross and four-sided stitches are worked in alternating colors (embroidered detail is illustrated at the right).

55 Embroidered detail of the alphabet pattern shown at the left. First, embroider the cross stitch section as illustrated on page 13, a through c. You may embroider the four-sided stitch on the front side so that the crosses are produced on the back. Or work in reverse and embroider the cross stitch on the front so that the four-sided stitch appears on the back. If this seems too difficult, you can use the simple cross and four-sided stitches (pages 11, 14 and 15).

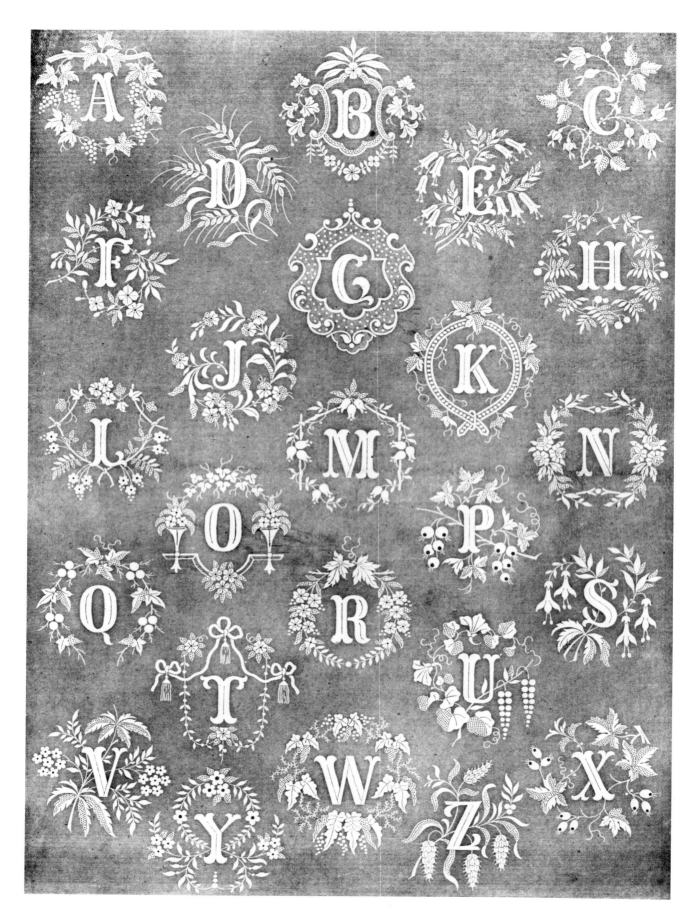

(Above) 57   Embroidered detail of the letter *W* from the adjoining alphabet, worked on coarse linen with various thicknesses of embroidery threads. The embroidery was worked in a round embroidery frame.

Using the enlarger of a photocopier, any single letter or the entire alphabet can be enlarged to suit your plan. To transfer letters onto the fabric, see pages 7 and 8.

(Opposite) 56   Letter designs for white embroidery from the 1867 issue of *Bazar* (embroidered detail is shown above).

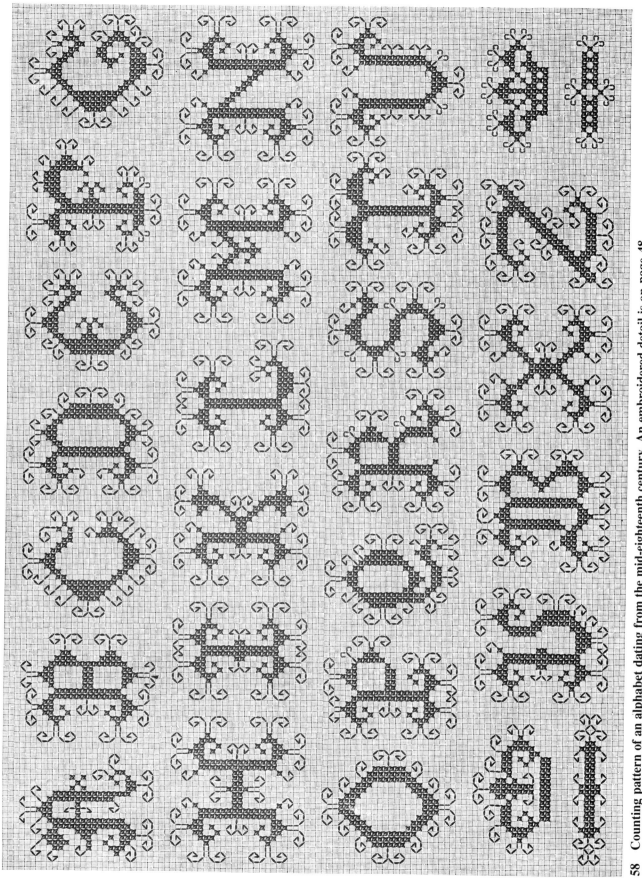

58 Counting pattern of an alphabet dating from the mid-eighteenth century. An embroidered detail is on page 48.

59 Counting pattern from *Bazar* magazine, circa 1850. Embroidered detail is on page 48.

(Above) 60   Embroidered detail for the alphabet on page 46.

(Above) **62** Two-colored alphabet sampler, embroidered from the counting pattern on page 50. The missing *I* can be reproduced from the *J* by embroidering the top and bottom of the left side on the right vertical section of the embroidery.

(Opposite) **61** Embroidered details of the alphabet on page 47. The complete embroidered alphabet is shown in color on the front cover and on page 20.

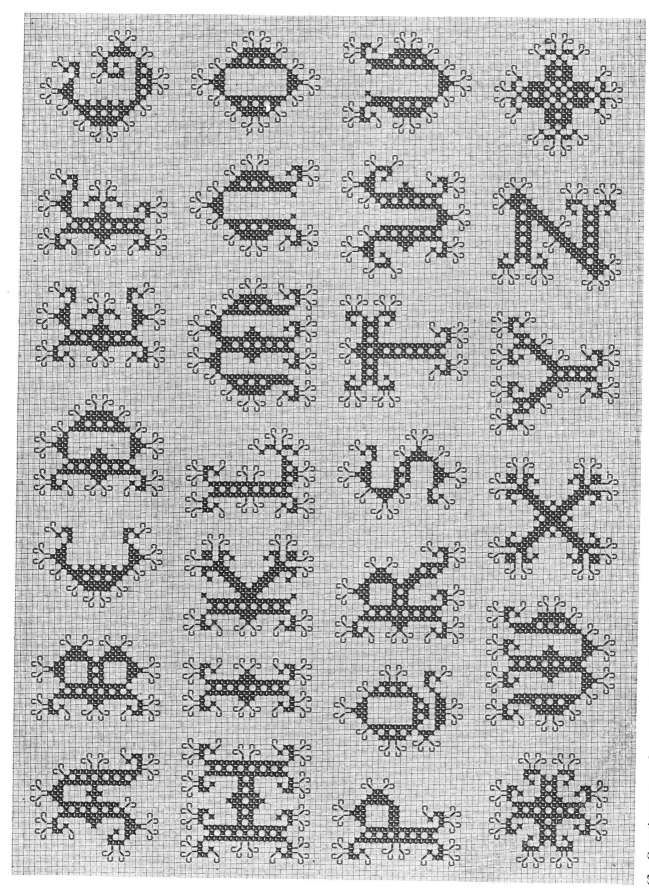

63 Counting pattern for a very decorative alphabet. An embroidered detail is on page 52 (top).

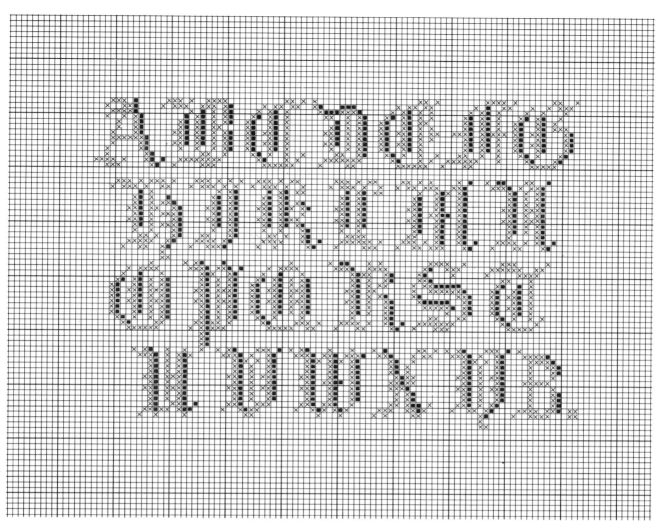

64 Counting pattern for an alphabet to be worked either in two colors or in two different stitches, cross stitch and four-sided stitch, for example. Symbols on the pattern marked as squares stand for either crosses in a contrasting color or for four-sided stitch embroidered in a contrasting color.

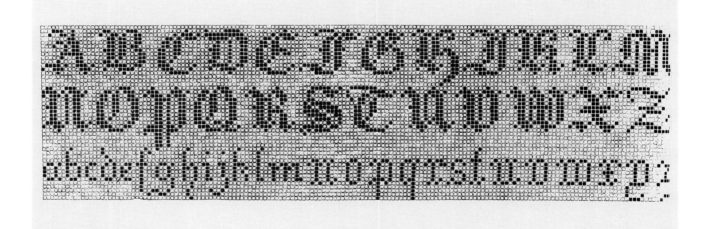

(Left) 65   Embroidered letters of the alphabet on page 50.

(Below) 66   Counting pattern for an alphabet from the magazine *Bazar* (circa 1850) with capitals and lowercase letters. Embroidered detail is below.

(Right) 67   Embroidered detail of the counting pattern shown above.

68   Old sampler of unknown origin. The omission of the missing letters indicates that it may be derived from Latin. The missing letters can be reproduced, if desired, from those illustrated: for example, the _K_ from the _R_; the _W_ from the _V_. Counting patterns for the alphabets (arranged in different order) are on pages 54 and 55.

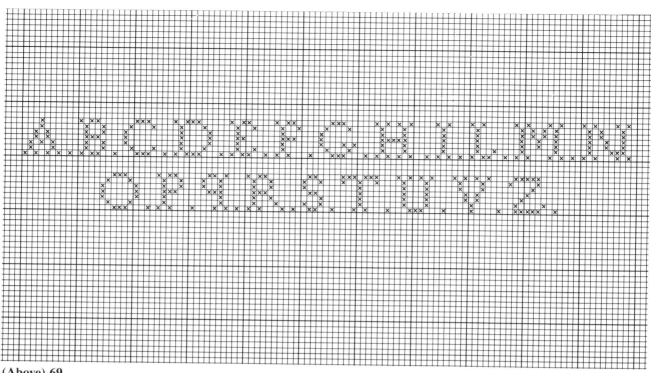

(Above) 69

(Below) 70

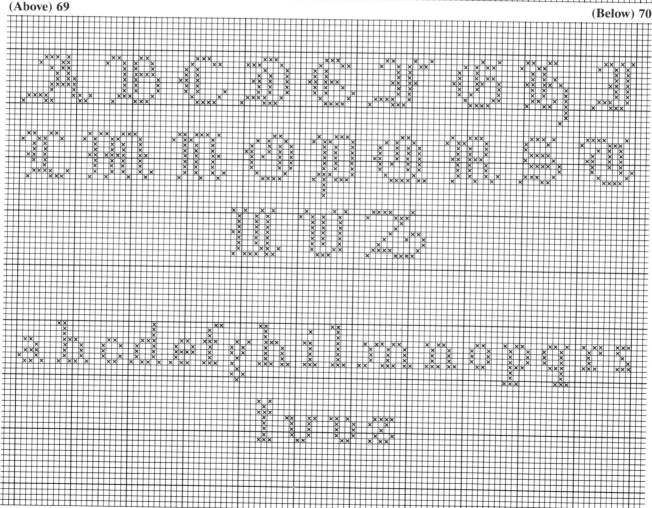

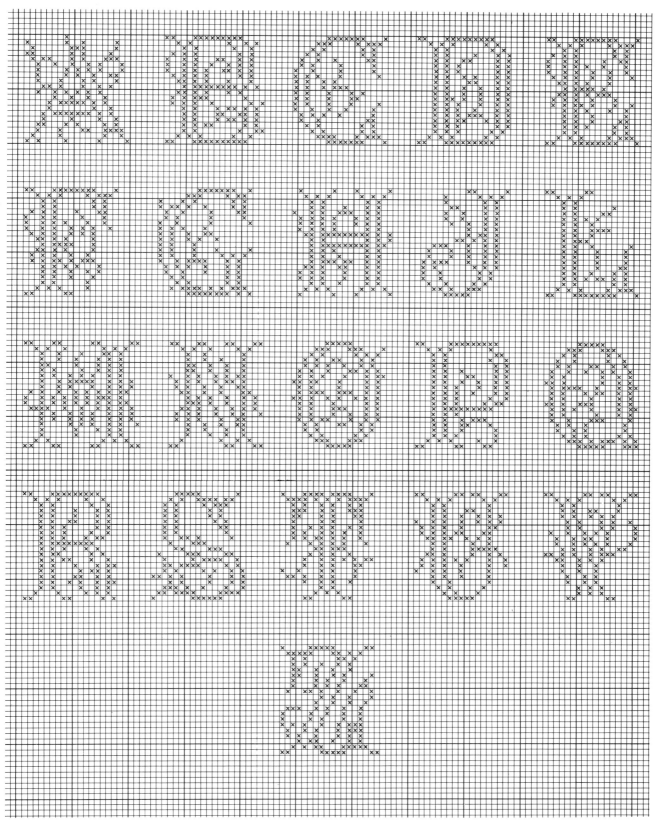

71

**Illustrations 69, 70 and 71 are counting patterns for the alphabet
sampler on page 53.**

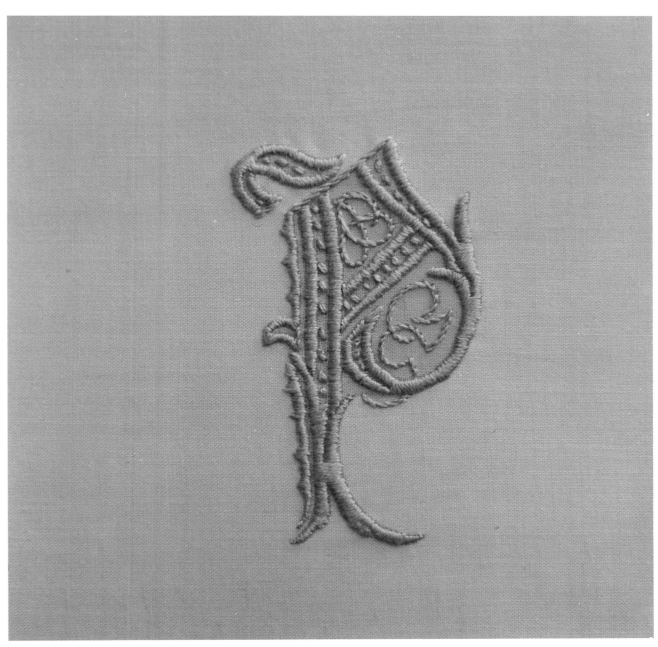

73 Embroidered letter of the alphabet on page 56. The alphabet was planned for white embroidery. It was adapted from a sampler illustrated in the magazine *Bazar* (nineteenth-century issue). The missing letter *I* can be made from the *L*. The letters can be enlarged (as described on page 10) and transferred onto the fabric (see pages 7 and 8).

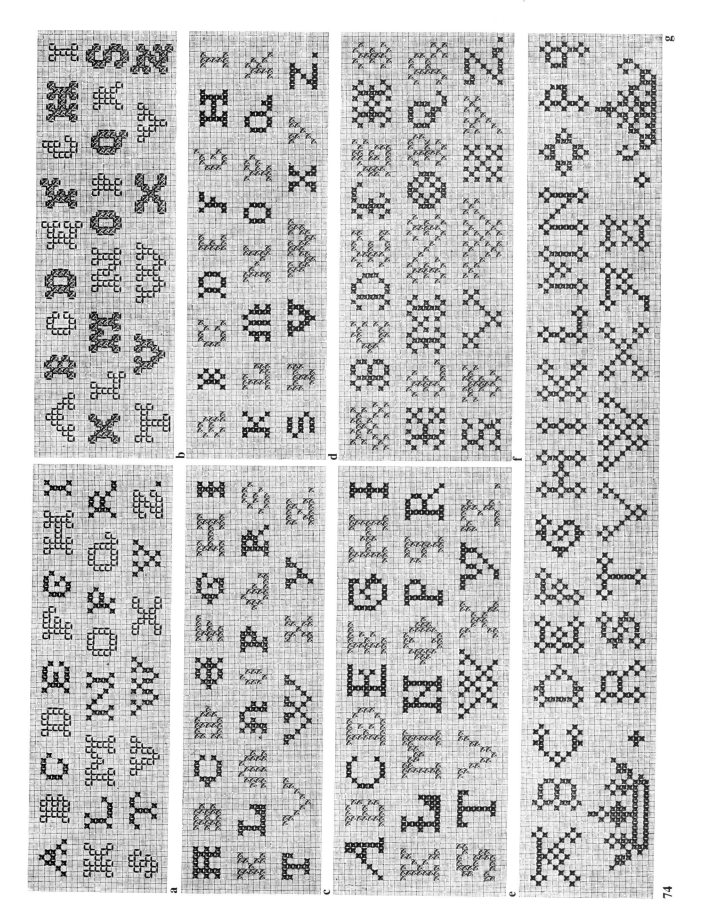

58

74

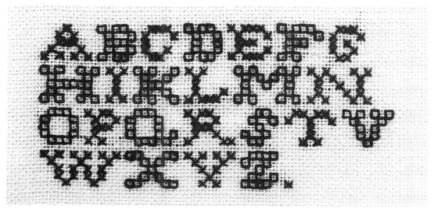

75a

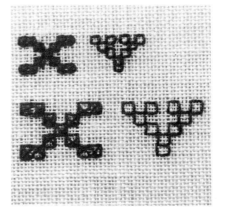

75b

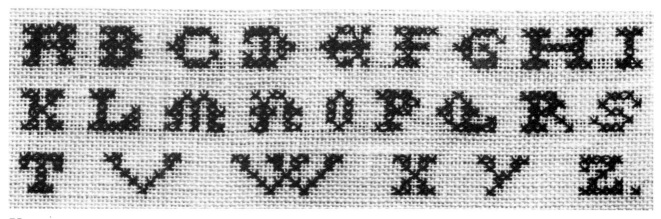

75c

75 a to c   Embroidered details of alphabets a, b and c from the
counting patterns on page 58. These alphabets come from a German
sampler, embroidered on linen, from *Modenwelt* magazine (1881).

   Detail a illustrates an alphabet alternating cross and four-sided
stitches.

   Detail b shows letters which were embroidered alternately in cross
stitch with double running or Holbein edging (the *X*) and in four-sided
stitch (the *Y*). It demonstrates the difference in stitch size resulting by
working over 2 or 3 threads of the evenweave fabric.

   Detail c shows a plain alphabet which is suitable to practice the two-
sided cross stitch technique (pages 11–13).

75d

75e

75f

75g

75 d to g   Sampler d shows a small, plain alphabet, suitable for embroidering entire names, words or sentences. Embroidered detail e shows three letters from alphabet e.

Embroidered detail f illustrates a very simple embroidery, plain letters that you can quickly embroider.

Detail g shows part of an alphabet which also is easy to work. You can use the two-sided cross stitch (pages 11–13) or the cross and four-sided stitch (pages 13–15). Counting patterns for these embroidered letters are on page 58.

76 Curved alphabet sampler, circa 1880, from the Engel Textile Museum, Hamburg. Embroidered on batiste fabric, the sampler is bordered with curved scallops and is predominately worked in satin and stem stitches (satin stitch, page 17; stem stitch, page 18). Drawing patterns of the alphabets are on pages 62 and 63.

(Above) 77 and (Below) 78 Drawing patterns for the alphabets from the curved alphabet sampler on page 61.

ABCDEFGHIJKLMN

OPQRSTUVWXYZ

abcdefghijklmnopqrstuvwxyz

abcdefghijklmnopqrstuvwxyz

79 Two alphabets embroidered from the counting pattern on page 65. Similar rows of letters were embroidered by children in their school handwork instruction at the turn of the century. Typically, the letters were done in red thread on cotton or linen fabric. For this sampler, rough linen was embroidered with Swedish linen thread (which, unfortunately, was not colorfast).

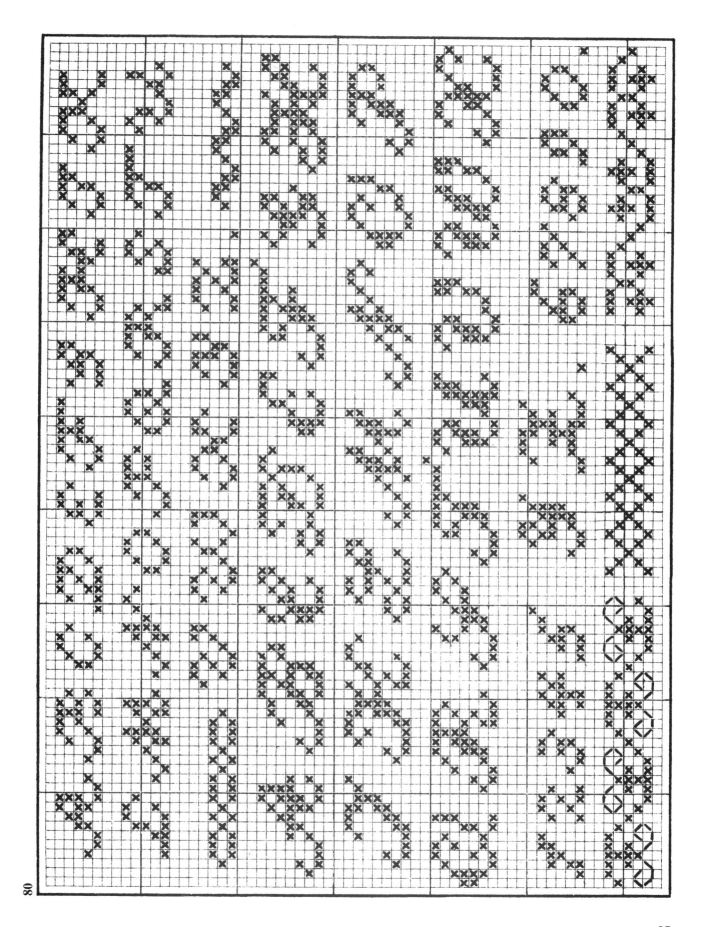

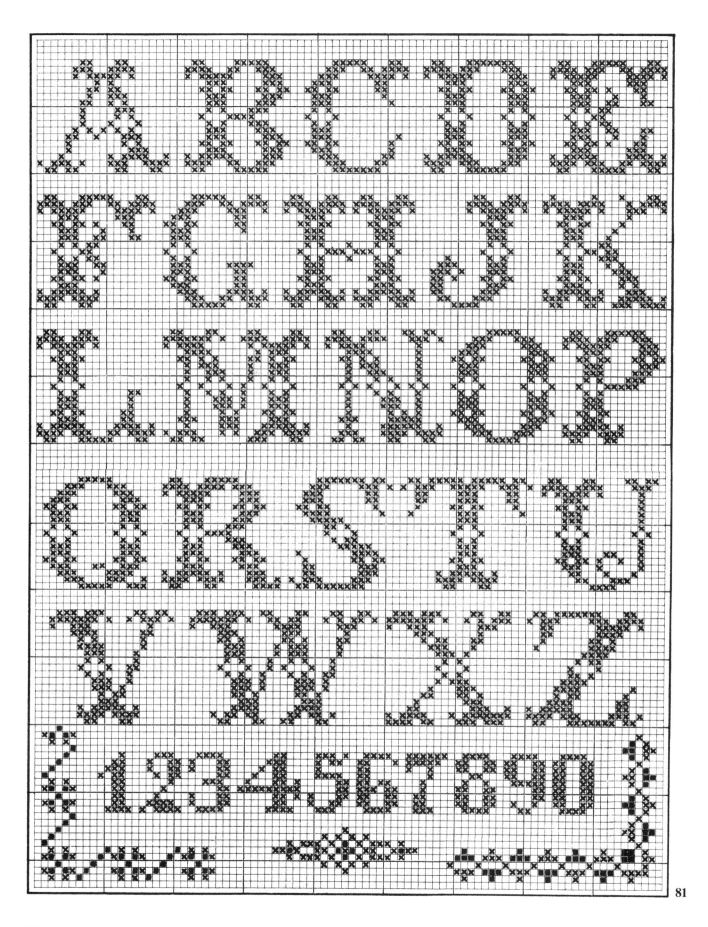

82 Embroidered cross stitch detail of the counting pattern on page 66.

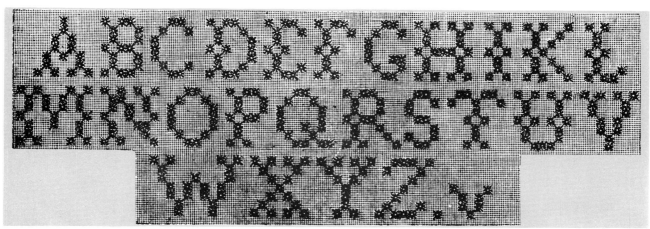

83 and 84 Alphabet and detail *A* embroidered in star eyelet stitch (the star eyelet stitch is described on page 16).

This alphabet also can be worked in two-sided cross stitch (page 15) or in simple cross stitch (page 11) although when embroidered in cross stitch, the letters will be very small.

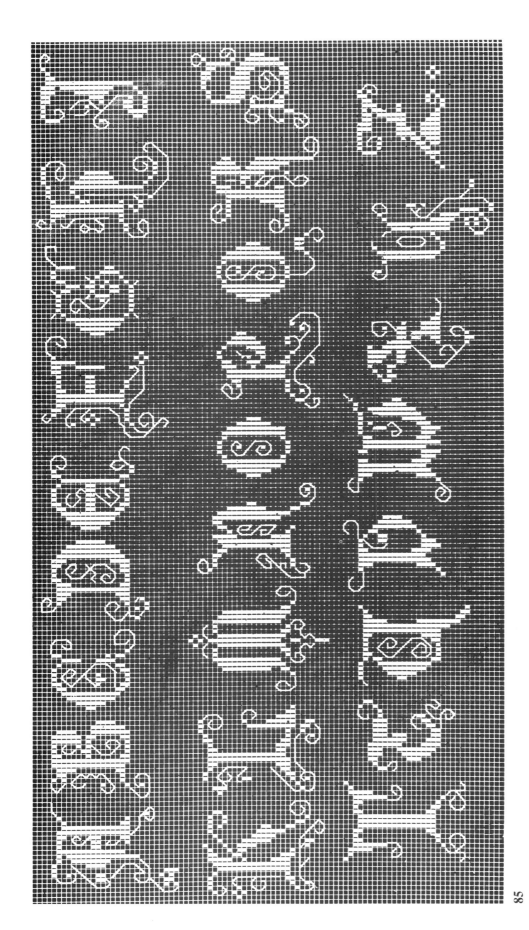

(Right) 86 Embroidered detail worked in cross stitch, decorated with straight stitches, from the alphabet on page 68. The counting pattern is from a mid-nineteenth-century issue of *Bazar* magazine.

In this counting pattern the *I* is missing; it can be reproduced from the letter *T* by changing the top and bottom.

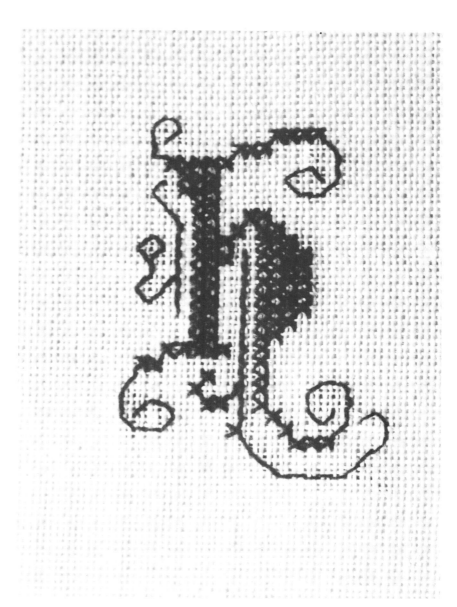

(Below) 87 Embroidered detail of the alphabet on page 70.

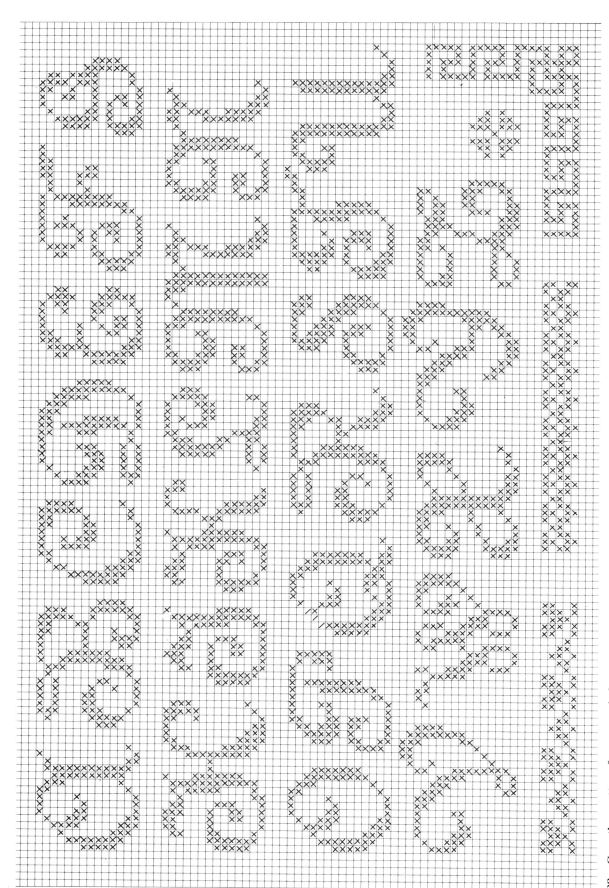

88 Counting pattern for a twentieth-century alphabet. A letter is missing here, too, as it frequently is in many samplers. An embroidered detail is on page 69.

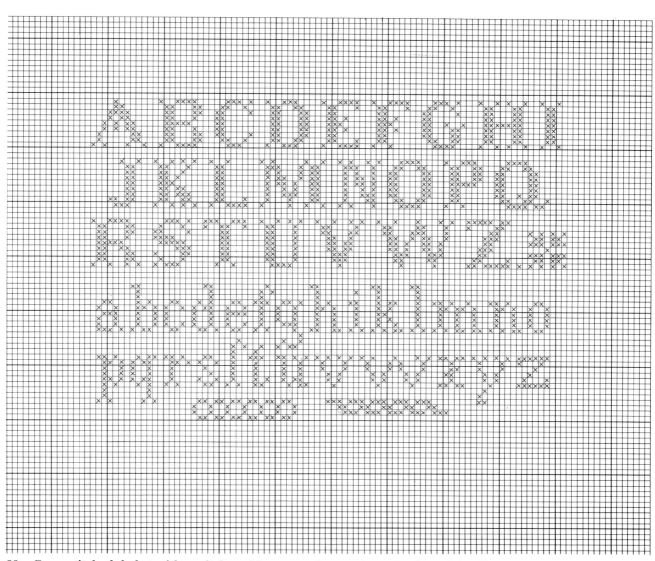

89 Cross stitch alphabet with capitals and lowercase letters. An embroidered detail is shown below.

90

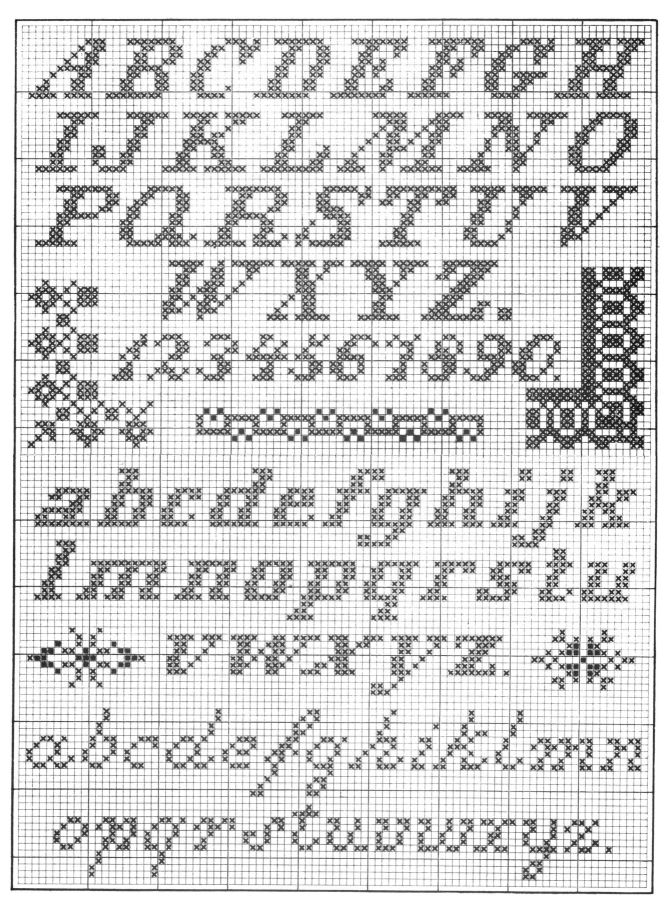

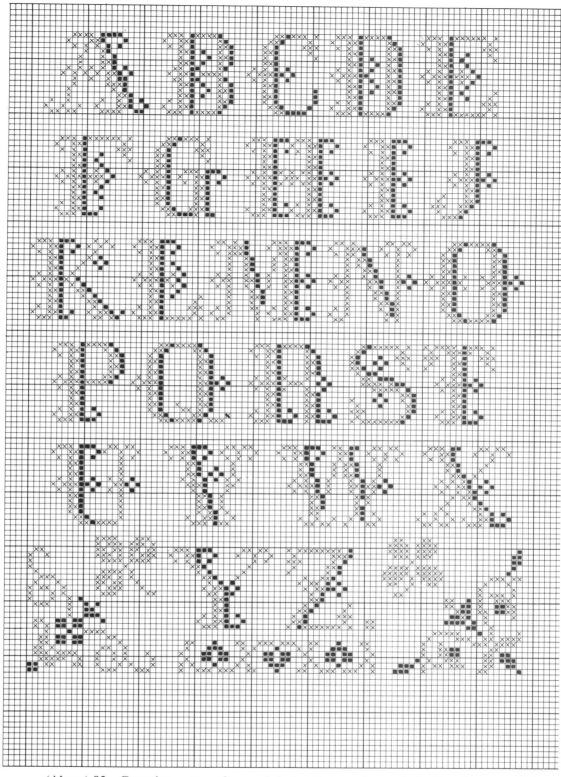

(Above) 92 Counting pattern for an alphabet that can be worked either in cross stitch or four-sided stitch (as in Illustration 94 on page 74) or in two colors using only cross stitch.

(Opposite) 91 Counting pattern with three alphabets and one row of numerals for cross stitch embroideries. An embroidered detail of this is shown at the top of page 74.

93 Embroidered detail of the counting pattern on page 72. The letters were embroidered with pearl cotton thread on coarse linen.

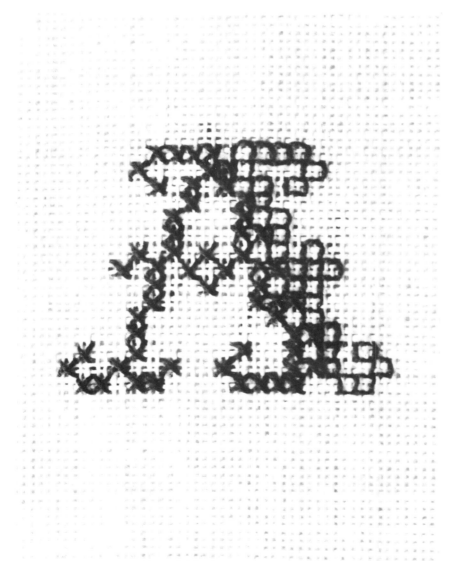

94 The letter *A* embroidered from the alphabet on page 73. You can embroider the letters as shown, in cross and four-sided stitches (pages 13–15). Experienced embroiderers, however, may prefer the two-sided cross stitch (pages 11–13), especially useful if the embroidery is to be viewed from both sides, as on an embroidered shawl.

95 These letters, easily adapted to initials, monograms or signatures, are especially large and decorative. The counting pattern of the entire alphabet is found on page 76. The alphabet illustrated here is derived from a German linen sampler, circa 1790, assembled in 1881 by *Modenwelt* magazine.

96 Counting pattern described on page 75.

Alphabet Patterns

97

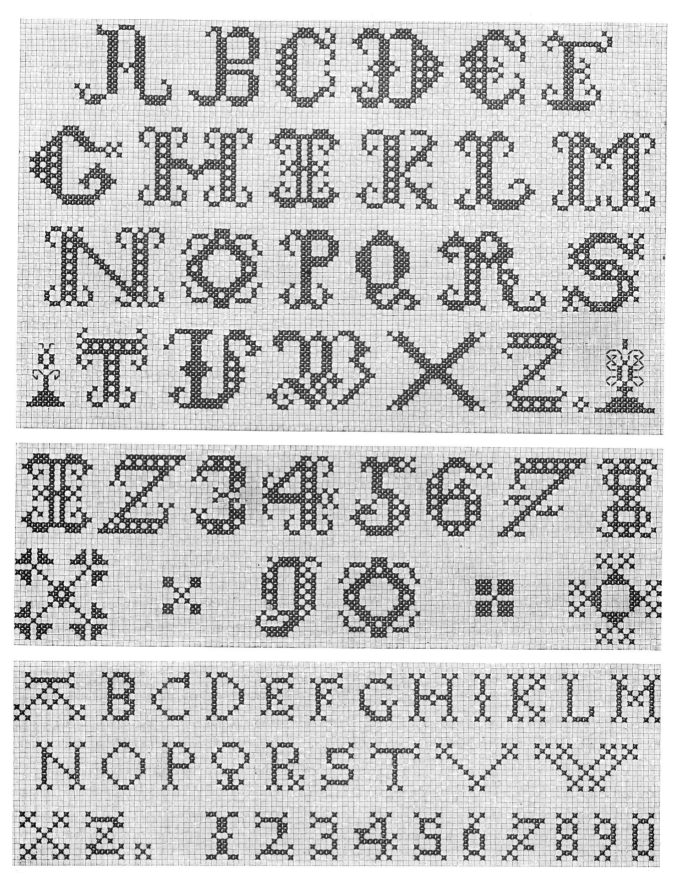

99

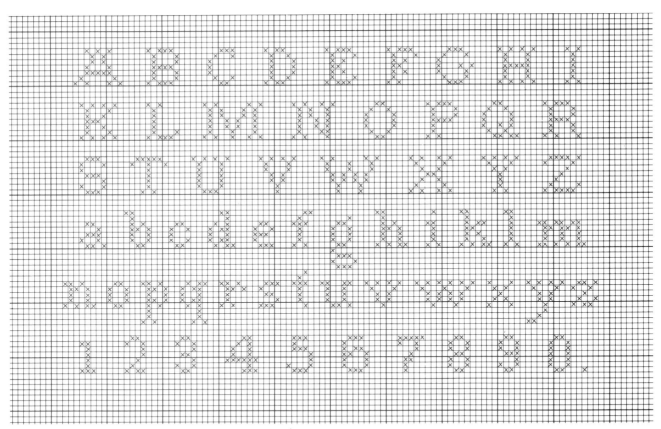

100

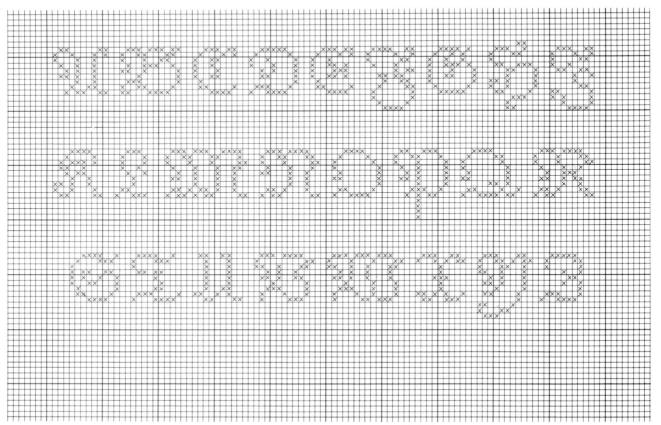

101

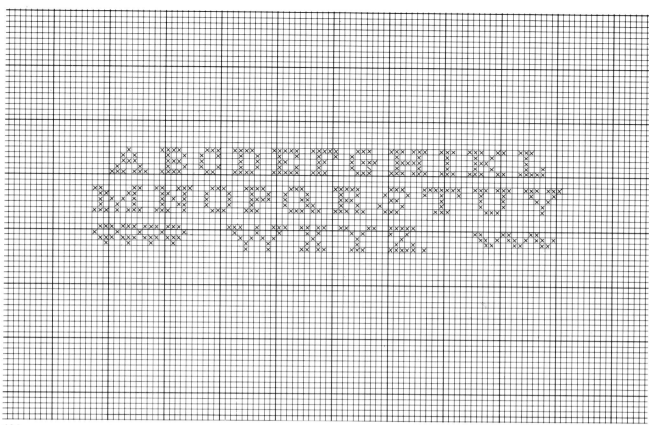

102

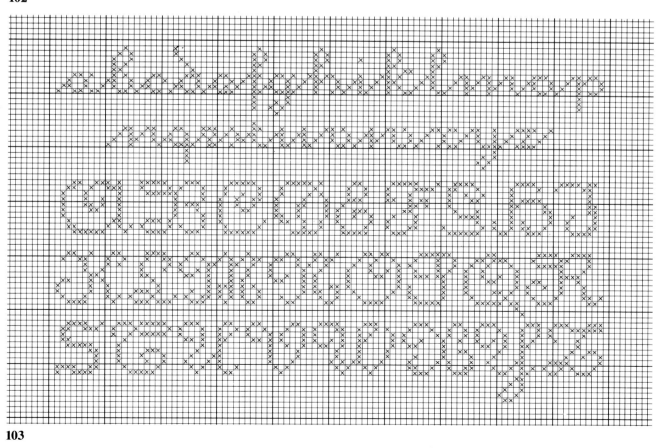

103

104

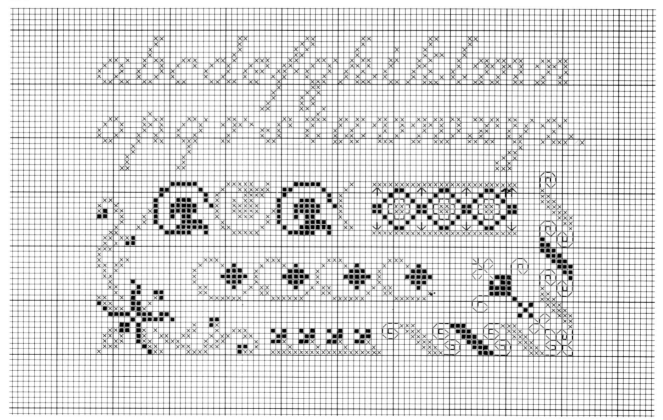

105

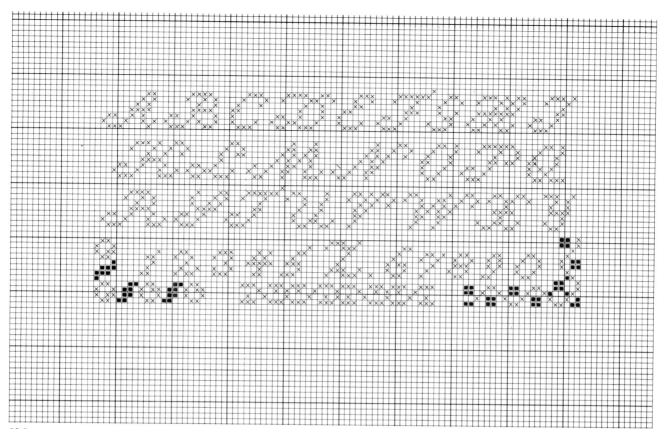

106

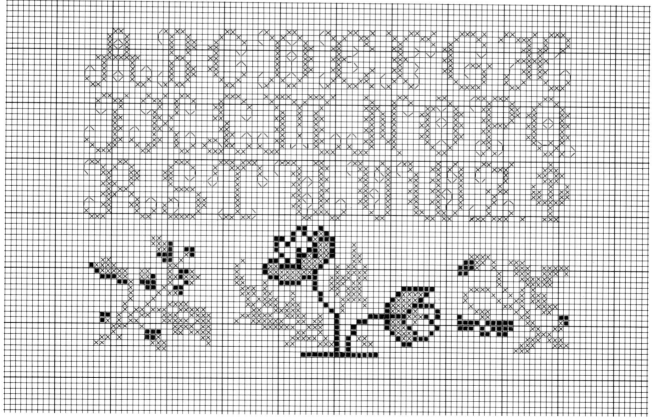

107

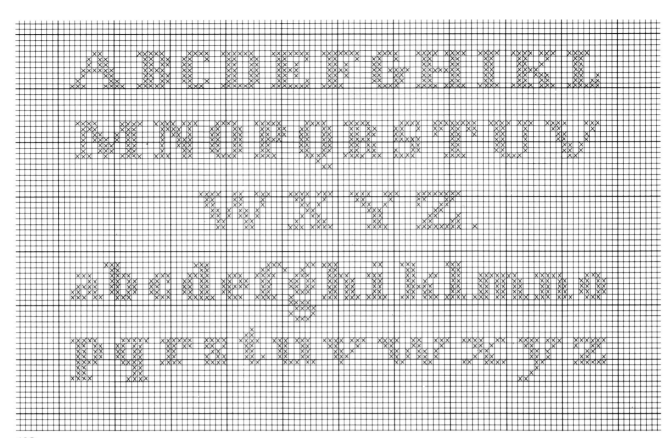

108

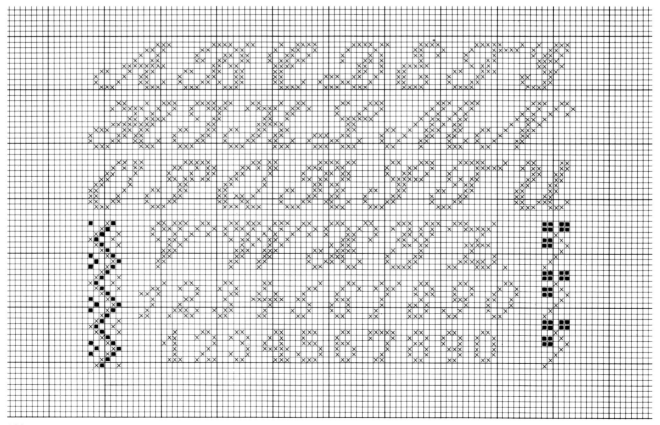

109

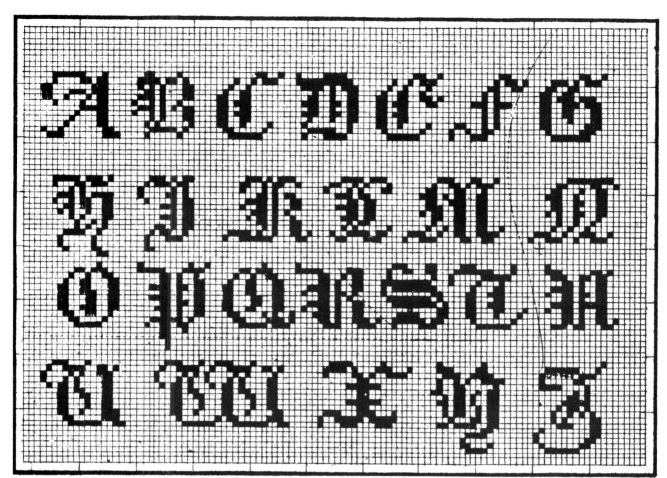

110

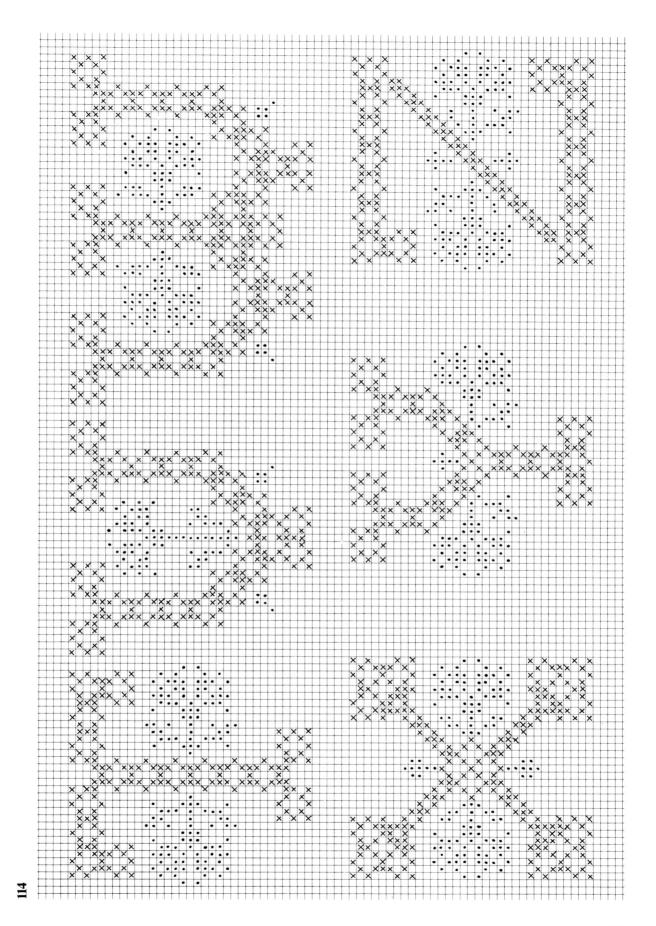

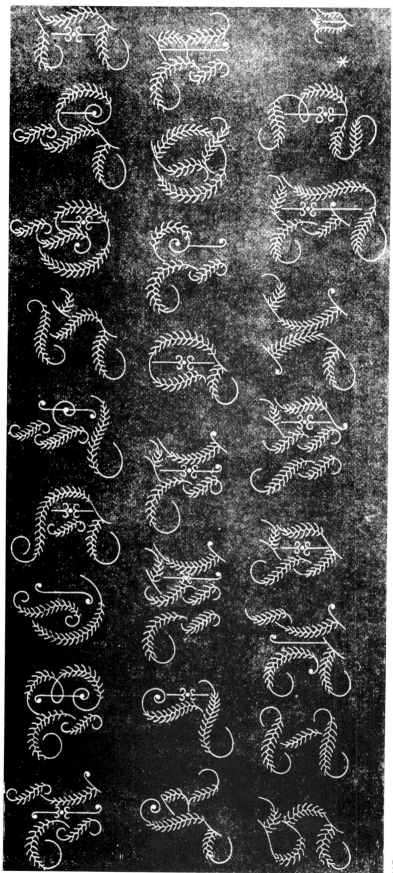

115

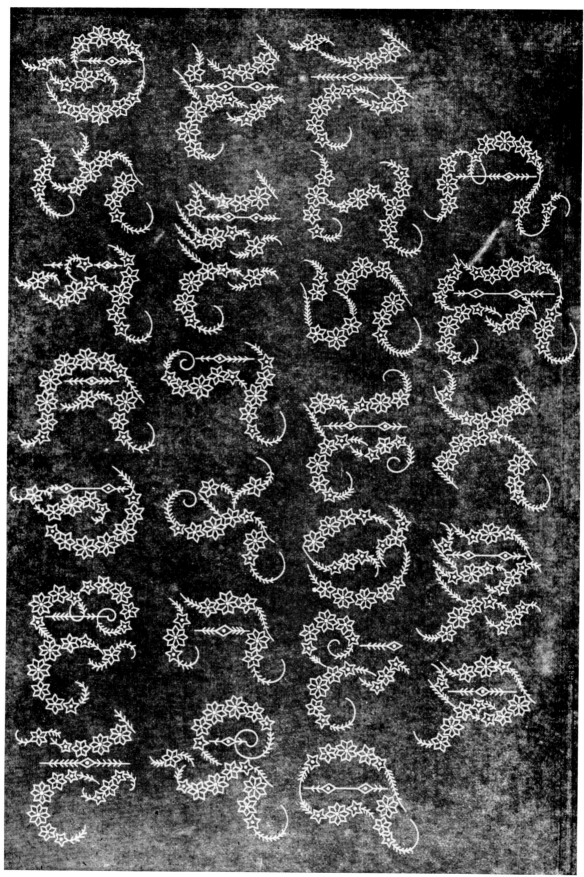

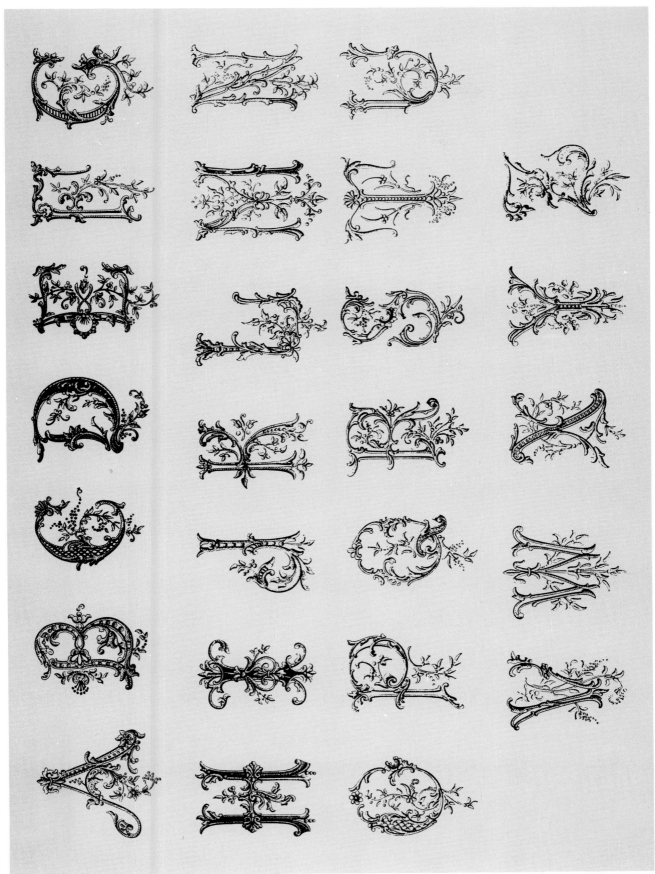

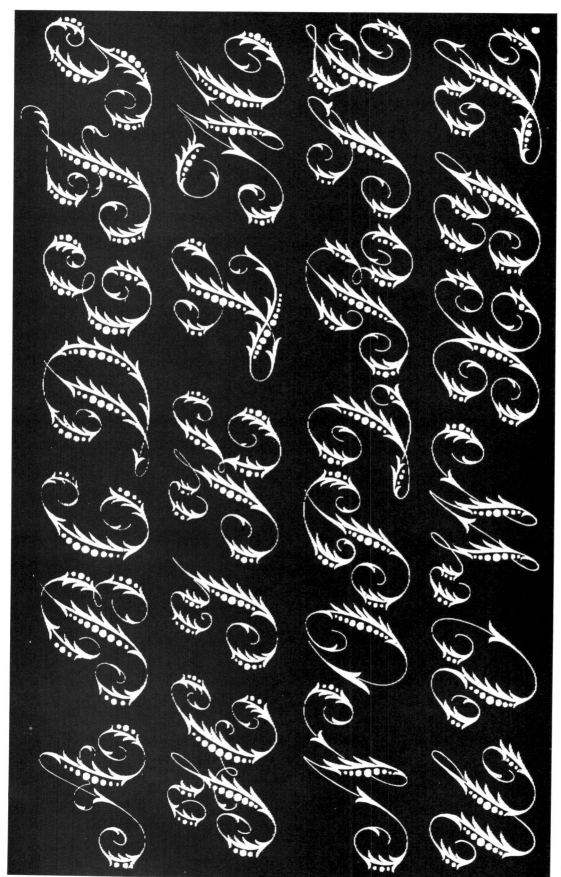

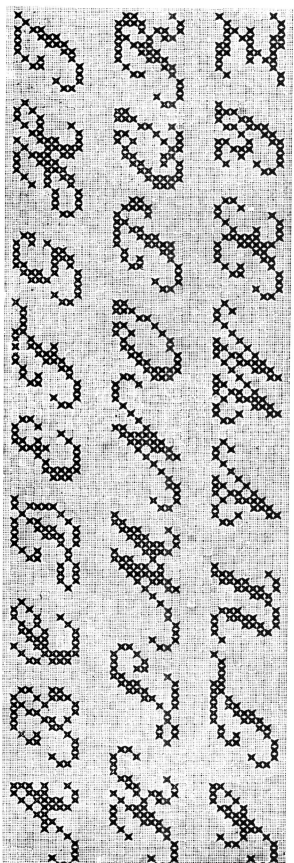

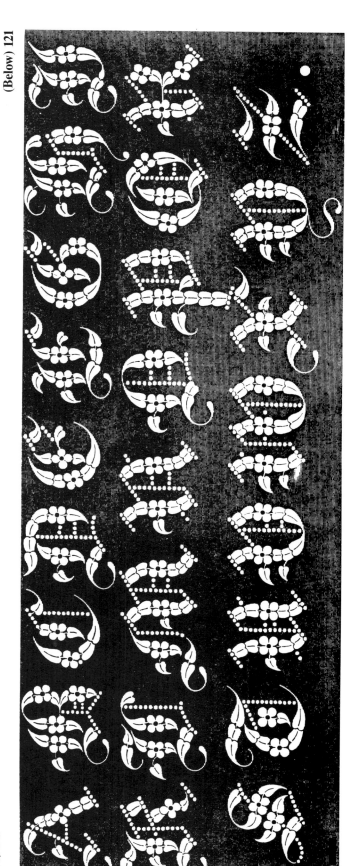

INDEX

(Page numbers in italics refer to illustrations.)